MIAMI
ART DECO

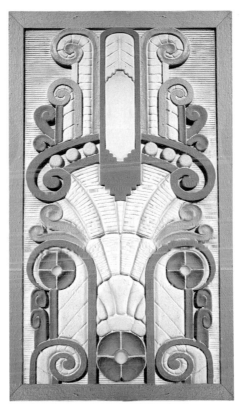

Washington Avenue looking South from 15th Street, Miami Beach, Florida

The Cameo Theatre, 1936,
1445 Washington Avenue.
Architect:
E. L. Robertson.

Previous page:
Stucco decoration,
Congress Hotel, 1936,
1052 Ocean Drive.
Architect:
Henry Hohauser.

MIAMI ART DECO

ARNOLD SCHWARTZMAN

Right:
Decorative relief,
Bentley Hotel, 1939,
Architects:
John & Carlton
Skinner.

Contents page:
Decorative stucco,
The Berkeley Shore,
1935,
1940 Park Avenue.
Architects:
Kiehnel & Elliott.

First published in 2023 by Palazzo Editions Ltd
15 Church Road
London, SW13 9HE
www.palazzoeditions.com

Text © 2023 Arnold Schwartzman
Design and layout copyright © 2023 Arnold Schwartzman

Paperback ISBN 9781786751317

Bound and printed in China

10 9 8 7 6 5 4 3 2 1

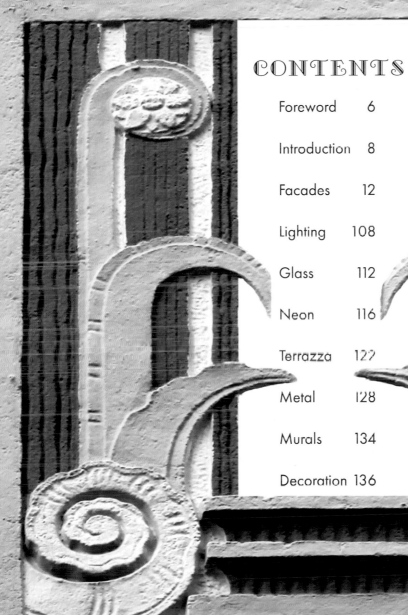
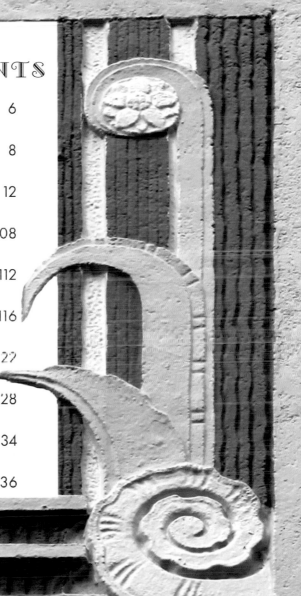

CONTENTS

When it comes to Art Deco, Miami Beach is a city of firsts. In 1976, Barbara Baer Capitman and Leonard Horowitz founded the Miami Design Preservation League (MDPL), the world's first Art Deco Society. Subsequently, Barbara Capitman, Michael Kinerk and Dennis Wilhelm traveled to cities in the USA, discovering Art Deco structures and encouraging interested locals to form their own Art Deco Societies. Today, 29 Art Deco Societies around the world are members of the International Coalition of Art Deco Societies (ICADS). All of them trace their lineage back to Miami Beach.

In 1979, MDPL was successful in getting the Art Deco Architectural District in Miami Beach listed on the National Register of Historic Places. This was the first historic district in the National Register devoted to 20th century architecture.

In 1991, MDPL hosted the first World Congress on Art Deco®, a brainchild of Barbara Capitman, who unfortunately didn't live to see it happen, as she passed in 1990 from congestive heart failure. In 1992, the idea that became ICADS was hatched at an Art Deco Symposium held in Miami Beach. World Congresses have been held in different cities around the world every 2 years, with the exception of the pandemic year of 2021.

In 2023, Miami Beach becomes the first city to host the World Congress twice.

Jack D. Johnson, Board Chair, Miami Design Preservation League

16TH WORLD CONGRESS
ON ART DECO
FLORIDA - USA

This book is provided by
Miami Design Preservation League

for

**THE 16TH WORLD CONGRESS ON ART DECO®:
MODERNISM – FLORIDA'S HIDDEN TREASURES**

April 18 – 30, 2023

Pre-Congress April 19 – 20   Central Florida

World Congress April 20 – 27   Miami Beach/Miami

Post-Congress April 28 – 30   Palm Beach County

Learn more at **MDPL.org** and **16thworldcongressonartdeco.com**

The Pastel Peninsular In 1976, writer, artist and preservationist Barbara Baer Capitman joined forces with New York designer and colorist Leonard Horowitz to establish the Miami Design Preservation League, covering over 800 buildings built from 1923–1943. In 1979, these structures were added to the National Register of Historic places.

New pastel color palates introduced by Horowitz complemented the areas' tropical green palms, pink flamingos and azure blue skies.

Natural disasters at opposite ends of the globe brought us two cities claiming to be the Art Deco capital of the World, New Zealand's city of Napier, which in 1931 experienced a devastating earthquake, and the hurricane-flattened city of Miami in 1926. Their destruction required the need to rebuild at a time when other parts of the world were benefitting from the architectural influence of the 1925 Paris expo. Both Napier and Miami adopted the Deco look, each adding their own characteristics. Among the most prolific Miami architects were Henry Hohauser, L. Murray Dixon, Albert Anis, Anton Skislewicz.

These architects adopted new materials that included reinforced concrete, stucco, stainless steel, aluminum, terazzo floors and bakelite, plus unique innovations such as "eyebrows" above windows to provide shade from Miami's tropical sun. Today many of Horowitz's pastel facades have reverted to their original white surfaces.

Memorial to
Barbara Baer
Capitman,
Lummus Park,
Miami Beach, FL.

Dreamland Cinema, 1935. Marine Terrace, Margate, UK. Architects: Leathert & Granger.

From Dreamland to Paradise I grew up in the British seaside town of Margate, where our family home was situated at the edge of the 1933 Art Deco Moderne Palm Bay Estate, and I frequently visited the town's 1935 Dreamland cinema. These two superb examples became my earliest appreciation of the Art Deco style.

Later, as an advertising agency art director during the 1970s, I was producing a number of commercials for the Coca-Cola company. On one occasion my choice of location was the island of Jamaica which required a stop-over at Miami.

On arrival at Miami airport, wishing to see the peninsular's unique form of architecture, I took a taxi to the Miami Beach district. Soon after reaching Collins Avenue, I realized that I was running out of time to make my connecting flight to Jamaica, thus I instructed the driver to return to the airport, allowing me to take only a few snaps out of the cab's windows!

My brief visit prevented me from learning that the district had fallen into serious disrepair plus the fact that some of its iconic structures had fallen victim to the wrecking ball.

It was to be another ten years before this unique area was blessed with the arrival of a guardian angel in the form of Barbara Baer Capitman, who joined forces with colorist Leonard Horowitz, to spearhead the creation of the Miami Design Preservation League.

Some 70 years after my first visit to Miami the opportunity arose once more to return to the district when I was invited to the Dominican Republic to receive a lifetime achievement award at the nation's Film Festival. Flying this time westward from my Hollywood home again required a stop in Miami, thus giving me the opportunity to spend a few exciting days photographing the district's numerous pastel palaces. My wife and I lodged at Ocean Drive's Breakwater Hotel where I noticed that directly opposite the hotel on the beach was the Moderne style Beach Patrol Headquarters. I suggested that we get up the next morning prior to sunrise. Our pre-breakfast wait for the morning sun was well worth the effort as can be observed in the following pages.

Wish you were here... Miami Beach's hotels provided their guests with free postcards with the view of advertising to a future clientele. The postcards took great creative license in constructing a false reality by selling their establishment within its own detached colorful gardens of palms and flora.

The largest printing company of these linen-finish paper postcards was Curt Teich & Co of Chicago, mostly known for its "Greetings from" cards of cities and towns across North America depicting travel, transportation, architecture etc., as well as for the hotel postcards it produced. Most of the Curt Teich postcards were printed by the C.T. Art Colortone.

Arnold Schwartzman OBE RDI, Hollywood 2023

*Beach Patrol
Headquarters, 1934,
1001 Ocean Drive.
Architect:
Robert A. Taylor.*

FACADES

Breakwater Hotel, 1939,
940 Ocean Drive.
Architect:
Anton Skislewicz.

14

Beacon Hotel, 1937,
720 Ocean Drive.
Architect:
Harry O. Nelson.

17

THE AVALON HOTEL ON OCEAN DRIVE
CORNER 7TH STREET
MIAMI BEACH, FLORIDA

Avalon Hotel, 1941,
700 Ocean Drive.
Architect:
Albert Anis.

Collins Avenue looking North from 11th Street,
Miami Beach, Florida

Tudor Hotel, 1939,
1111 Collins Avenue.
Architect:
L. Murray Dixon.

Tiffany Hotel, 1939,
801 Collins Avenue.
Architect:
L. Murray Dixon.

Signage,
Victor Hotel, 1937,
1144 Ocean Drive.
Architect:
L. Murray Dixon.

Signage,
Paris Cinema, 1946,
550 Washington Ave.
Architect:
Henry Hohauser.

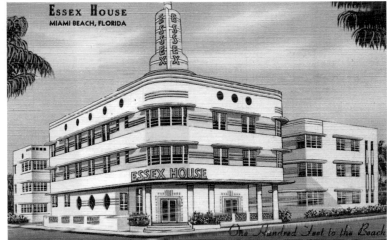

Essex House, 1938,
1001 Collins Avenue.
Architect:
Henry Hohauser,

27

HALF BLOCK FROM OCEAN

9A-H2426

Kent Hotel, 1939,
1131 Collins Avenue.
Architect:
L. Murray Dixon.

PALMER HOUSE
Half Block from Ocean
MIAMI BEACH, FLORIDA

Palmer House, 1939,
1119 Collins Avenue.
Architect:
L. Murray Dixon.

Barbizon Apartments, 1937,
556 Ocean Drive.
Architect:
John Coulton Skinner.

SHERBROOKE
HOTEL APARTMENTS

100 FEET TO OCEAN
MIAMI BEACH, FLORIDA

Sherbrooke Apartments, 1947,
901 Collins Avenue.
Architects:
MacKay & Gibbs.

Signage, Sherbrooke Hotel, 1947, 901 Collins Ave. Architects: MacKay & Gibbs.

HOTEL SHELLEY

HOTEL LA SALLE, MIAMI BEACH, FLORIDA

Hotel Shelley, 1931,
formerly Hotel La Salle,
844 Collins Avenue.
Architect:
Henry J. Maloney.

Hotel Webster, 1939,
currently a clothing store,
1220 Collins Avenue.
Architect:
Henry Holhauser.

HOTEL CHESTERFIELD. COLLINS AVE. AT 9TH ST.
MIAMI BEACH, FLA.

Chesterfield Hotel, 1938,
855 Collins Avenue.
Architect:
Albert Anis.

Henrosa Hotel, 1935
formerly Biarritz Hotel,
1435 Collins Avenue.
Architect:
Harry O. Nelson.

McAlpin Hotel, 1940,
1424 Ocean Drive.
Architect:
L. Murray Dixon.

The Taft Hotel   Miami Beach, Florida

Hotel Taft, 1936,
1040 Washington Avenue.
Architect:
Henry Hohauser.

48

Pelican Hotel, 1948,
826 Ocean Drive.
Architect:
Renzo Rosso.

50

The Penguin Hotel, 1948,
1418 Ocean Drive.
Architect:
Henry Hohauser.

CRESCENT HOTEL   MIAMI BEACH, FLORIDA

CRESCENT

FACING OCEAN

Crescent Hotel, 1938,
1420 Ocean Drive.
Architect:
Henry Hohauser.

1430 OCEAN DRIVE—MIAMI BEACH, FLORIDA

Clyde

THE CLYDE — YOUR HOTEL — YOUR HOME — WINTER AND SUMMER

Ocean Plaza Hotel, 1941,
formerly Clyde Hotel,
1430 Ocean Drive.
Architect:
L. Murray Dixon.

Leslie Hotel, 1937,
1244 Ocean Drive.
Architect: Albert Anis.

Hotel Bancroft, 1939,
1501 Collins Avenue.
Architect:
Albert Anis.

THE CARLYLE
On the Ocean
Miami Beach, Florida

The Carlyle, 1941,
1250 Ocean Drive.
Architects:
Kichnell & Elliott.

HOTEL CARDOZO 1300 OCEAN DRIVE, MIAMI BEACH, FLORIDA

Hotel Cardozo, 1939,
1300 Ocean Drive.
Architect:
Henry Hohauser.

HOTEL IMPERIAL,
ON THE OCEAN AT 7TH STREET.
MIAMI BEACH. FLORIDA

IMPERIAL HOTEL

Hotel Imperial, 1939,
650 Ocean Drive.
Architect:
L. Murray Dixon.

HADDON HALL   FACING THE OCEAN

Haddon Hall Hotel, 1941,
1500 Collins Avenue.
Architect:
L. Murray Dixon.
Fountain sculptor:
Robert R. Schwarz.

70

Congress Hotel, 1936,
1052 Ocean Drive.
Architect: Henry Hohauser.

COLONY HOTEL 736 OCEAN DRIVE MIAMI BEACH, FLORIDA

ON THE OCEAN

Colony Hotel, 1935,
736 Ocean Drive.
Architect:
Henry Hohauser.

AIR-CONDITIONED ROOMS
WALDORF TOWERS HOTELS
On the Ocean at 9th Street
MIAMI BEACH, FLORIDA

The Waldorf Towers, 1937,
860 Ocean Drive.
Architect:
Albert Anis.

Park Central Hotel, 1937,
640 Ocean Drive.
Architect:
Henry Hohauser.

77

Cavalier Hotel, 1936,
1320 Ocean Drive.
Architect:
Roy F. France.

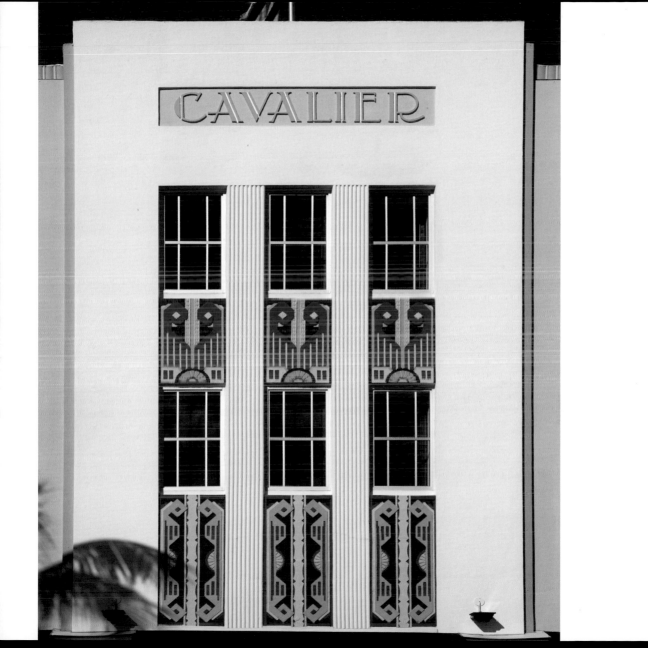

St. Moritz, 1939,
1565 Collins Avenue.
Architect:
L. Murray Dixon.

Delano Hotel, 1947,
1685 Collins Avenue.
Architect:
D. Robert Swartburg.

*Delano Hotel, 1947,
1685
Collins Avenue.
Architect:
D. Robert Swartburg.*

THE SHORECREST   MIAMI BEACH, FLORIDA

OUR OWN PRIVATE BEACH

Shorecrest Hotel, 1940,
1535 Collins Avenue.
Architects:
Kiehnell & Elliott.

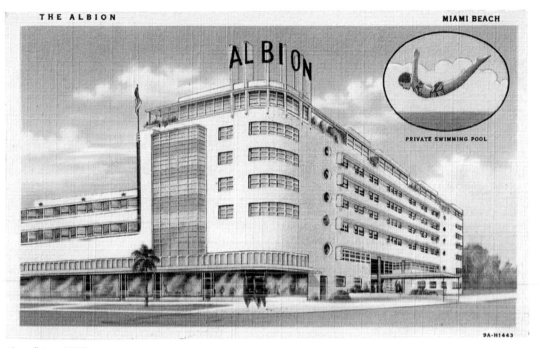

THE ALBION   MIAMI BEACH

ALBION

PRIVATE SWIMMING POOL

9A-H1443

The Albion, 1939,
1650 James Avenue.
Architect:
Igor Polovitzky.

Marseilles Hotel, 1947,
1741 Collins Avenue.
Architect:
Robert Swarthburg.

National Hotel, 1940,
1677 Collins Avenue.
Architect:
Roy F. France.

Sagamore Hotel, 1948,
1671 Collins Avenue.
Architect:
Albert Anis.

Sherborne Hotel, 1940,
1801 Collins Avenue.
Architect:
Igor Polevitzky.

Ritz Plaza, 1939,
formerly Grossinger,
currently SLS Hotel,
1701 Collins Avenue.
Architect:
L. Murray Dixon.

*Private residence
facade and relief,
1940,
Miami Beach, FL.
Sculptor:
Robert Swartburg.*

Private residence,
1100 14th Street,
Miami Beach, FL.

Hoffman's Cafeteria, 1939, currently Señor Frogs. 1450 Collins Avenue. Architect: Henry Hohauser.

ORIGINAL HOFFMAN'S   MIAMI BEACH, FLORIDA

HOFFMANS CAFETERIA

ORIGINAL

1450 COLLINS AVE. AT ESPANOLA WAY

12111

Hoffman's Cafeteria, 1939,
currently Senor Frogs,
1450 Collins Avenue.
Architect:
Henry Hohauser.

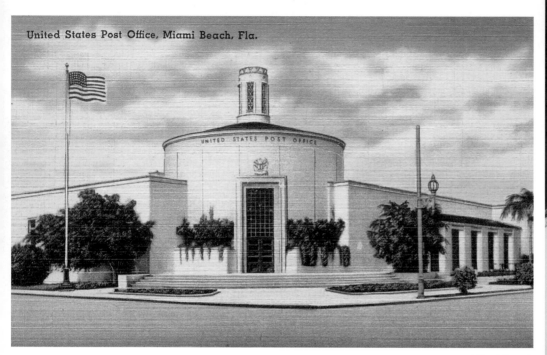

United States Post Office, Miami Beach, Fla.

Miami Beach
U.S. Post Office, 1939.
1300 Washington Avenue.
Architect:
Howard L. Cheney.

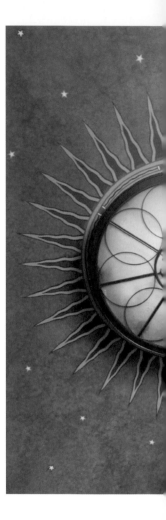

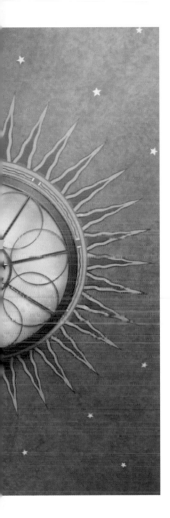

Left and right:
*Light fixtures,
Victor Hotel, 1937,
1144 Ocean Drive.
Architect:
L. Murray Dixon.*

Center:
*Light fixture,
Miami Beach Main
Post Office, 1939.
1300 Washington
Avenue.
Muralist:
Charles Hardman.*

109

Exterior light fixture,
Hotel Arlington,
455 Ocean Drive.
Late 1930s.
Architect:
Albert Anis.

THE OCEAN AT OUR DOOR

*Etched glass screen,
Hoffmans Cafeteria,
1939, currently
Señor Frogs.
1450 Collins Avenue.
Architect:
Henry Hohauser.*

Etched glass window, Tiffany Hotel, 1939. 801 Collins Avenue. Architect: L. Murray Dixon.

114

Etched glass,
*Beacon Hotel, 1937,
720 Ocean Drive.
Architect:
Harry O. Nelson.*

NEON

Neon sign,
Cadet Hotel, 1941,
1701 James Ave.
Architect:
Albert Anis.

Neon sign,
11th Street Diner,
1065
Washington Avenue,
Paramount Dining
Car Company.

Neon sign,
The Cameo
Theatre, 1936,
1445
Washington
Avenue.
Architect:
E. L. Robertson.

Right:
EdisonHotel, 1935,
960 Ocean Drive.
Architect:
Henry Hohauser.

Center:
Facade,
Breakwater
Hotel, 1939,
940 Ocean Drive.
Architect:
Anton Skislewicz.

Far right:
Essex House, 1938,
1001 Collins Ave.
Architect:
Henry Hohauser.

120

TERRAZZO

AIR-CONDITIONED ROOMS
VICTOR HOTEL
On the Ocean at 12th St.
MIAMI BEACH, FLORIDA

Opposite:
Detail,
terrazzo floor,
Victor Hotel, 1937,
1144 Ocean Drive.
Architect:
L. Murray Dixon.
Muralist:
Earl LaPan.

THE CLEVELANDER   MIAMI BEACH, FLORIDA

Directly On The Ocean

Clevelander Hotel, 1938,
1020 Ocean Drive.
Architect:
Albert Anis.

126

METALWORK

Opposite:
Railing,
Sherbrooke Hotel,
1947,
901 Collins Ave.
Architects:
MacKay & Gibbs.

This page:
Railings,
Marlin Hotel, 1939,
1200 Collins Ave.
Architect:
L. Murray Dixon.

*Seahorse
stair rails.
Private residence,
Miami Beach, FL.*

Metal screendoor,
private residence,
1015 13th Sreet,
Miami Beach, FL.

This page:
*Courtyard
staircase,*
and opposite:
*Facade,
The Parc Vendome
apartment
building, 1936,
736 13th Street.*
Architect:
Henry Hohauser.

Opposite:
Detail, murals,
Plymouth Hotel,
1940,
336 21st Street.
Architect:
Anton Skislewicz.
Muralist:
Ramon Chatov.

134

Decorative frieze,
Cameo Theatre,
1936,
1445 Washington
Avenue.
Architect:
E. L. Robertson.

SURF HOTEL

MIAMI BEACH, FLORIDA

SURF HOTEL

On the Oceanfront

7A-H2945

*Surf Hotel, 1936
(now a restaurant),
444 Ocean Drive.
Architect:
Henry Hohauser.*

THE MAYFAIR · MIAMI BEACH, FLORIDA · AT THE GOLF COURSE

Detail,
stucco facade,
The Mayfair, 1936,
1960 Park Avenue.
Architect:
Henry Hohauser.

*Fish and seaweed
stucco decoration,
Marlin Hotel, 1939,
1200 Collins Ave.
Architect:
L. Murray Dixon.*

Miami Beach High School, 1926, Drexel Avenue and 16th Street, now the Fienberg-Fisher K-8 School. Architect: August Geiger.

Bas relief,
Bass Museum, 1939,
2100 Collins Ave.
Architect:
Russel Pancoast.
Sculptor:
Gustav Bohland.
Pancoast.
Sculptor:
Gustav Bohland.

145

*Bas relief,
Bass Museum, 1939,
2100
Collins Avenue.
Architect:
Russel Pancoast.
Sculptor:
Gustav Bohland.
Pancoast.
Sculptor:
Gustav Bohland.*

*Wall decoration,
659 Washington
Avenue.*

THE ABBEY HOTEL   MIAMI BEACH, FLA.

Abbey Hotel, 1940,
300 21st Street.
Architect:
Albert Anis.

Overleaf:
Classical Revival
decorative detail,
The Franklin Hotel, 1934,
860 Collins Avenue.
Architect:
Victor Hugo Nellenbogen.

THE BERKELEY SHORE
MIAMI BEACH

The Berkeley Shore, 1935,
1940 Park Avenue.
Architects:
Kiehnel & Elliott.
Right:
detail,
stucco decoration.

*Stucco decoration,
Hotel Netherland
Apartments, 1935.
Architects:
Robertson& Patterson.*

Detail,
decorative stucco,
Cavalier Hotel,
1936,
1320 Ocean
Drive.
Architect:
Roy F. France.

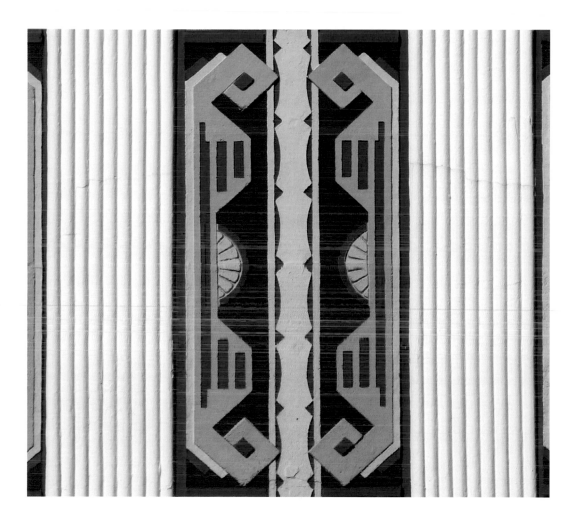

Arnold Schwartzman, OBE RDI, London-born, is a graphic designer, author, and the Academy Award®-winning documentary film producer/director of *Genocide* (1981). He is the author of a number of books, including *DECO LAndmarks, Art Deco Gems of Los Angeles* (2005), *London Art Deco* (2013), *Griffith Observatory, A Celebration of its Architectural Splendor* (2015), *Art Deco City* (2018) and *Paris Art Deco* (2023).

He was appointed the Director of Design for the 1984 Los Angeles Olympic Games. Among his recent design projects are two murals for Cunard's *MS Queen Elizabeth*, and the *U.N. Peace Bell Monument* in Seoul, South Korea.

In 2002, Schwartzman was appointed an Officer of the Order of the British Empire (OBE) by Queen Elizabeth II, and in 2006 was conferred the distinction of Royal Designer (RDI) by Britain's Royal Society of Arts. Arnold lives in Los Angeles, and works in collaboration with Isolde, his wife and creative partner.